SCHOLASTIC READER

LEVEL 3
700-1500 WORDS

W9-AXU-487

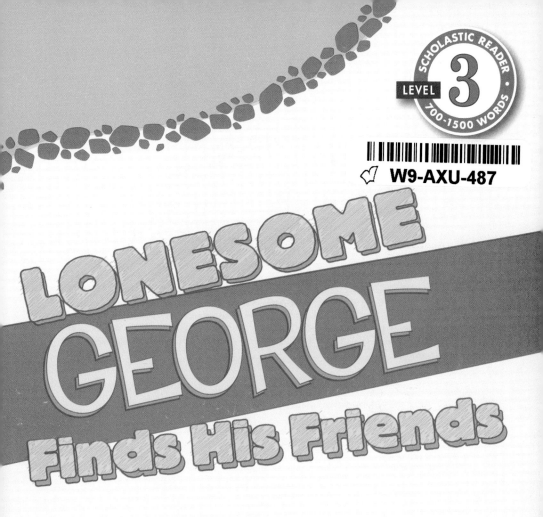

LONESOME GEORGE
Finds His Friends

By Tori Kosara

SCHOLASTIC INC.

New York   Toronto   London   Auckland
Sydney   Mexico City   New Delhi   Hong Kong

To KLE
Thank you, always!

Photo Credits

Front cover: ©Kevin Schafer/Alamy; back cover: ©Tier Und Naturfotografie J & C Sohns/Getty Images; p. 3: ©Javarman/ Shutterstock; p. 4: ©Rolf Richardson/Getty Images, (inset) ©Javarman/Shutterstock; p. 6: ©Michael Zysman/Shutter- stock; p. 7: ©Steve Allen (RF)/Getty Images; pp. 8-9: ©Alan Brookstone/Shutterstock; pp. 10-11: ©Eric Isselée/Shutter- stock, (inset) ©Brandon Cole Marine Photography/Alamy; p. 12: ©ArchMan/Shutterstock; p. 13: ©leospek/Shutterstock; p. 14: ©Peter Nicholson/Alamy; p. 15: ©Michael DeFreitas/Danita Delimont, Agent/Alamy; pp. 16-17: © blickwinkel/Maywald/Alamy; p. 18: ©Valeranda Media/Shutterstock; p. 19: ©DEA/C.DANI/I.JESKE/Contributor/Getty Images; pp. 20-21: ©INTERFOTO/ Alamy, (inset) ©Tier Und Naturfotografie J & C Sohns/Getty Images; p. 22: ©Panoramic Images/Getty Images; p. 23: ©Green Stock Media/Alamy; p. 24: ©Clara/Shutterstock; p. 25: ©Oxford Scientific/Photolibrary/Getty Images; p. 26: ©Doug Lemke/Shutterstock; p. 27: ©Javarman/Shutterstock; p. 28: ©David Madison/The Image Bank/Getty Images; p. 29: ©Arie v.d. Wolde/Shutterstock; pp. 30-31: © AridOcean/Shutterstock, (inset) ©Eric Rorer/Getty Images; p. 32: ©Eric Rorer/Getty Images.

Designed by: Marissa Asuncion

ISBN 978-0-545-26129-6

12 11 10 9 8 7 6 5 4 3 2 1   10 11 12 13 14 15/0

Printed in the U.S.A. 40
First printing, September 2010

I am Lonesome George. I am a giant Galápagos tortoise from the island of Pinta. I am almost one hundred years old!

The Galápagos tortoise is one of the largest types of tortoises on the planet. Some have weighed over 500 pounds (227 kilograms)!

I live on the Galápagos Islands. I am the only tortoise of my kind left here. Sometimes it gets lonely. But there are lots of other animals living on the Galápagos.

Because I am cold-blooded, I feel chilly when I wake up. I need the sun to warm me. When I go to the beach, I meet a young Galápagos sea lion. When he is not swimming he likes to sun on the shore, too.

When I am done warming up, I look around the beach. There are a lot of animals to see. This is a sea turtle. We may look alike, but sea turtles spend almost their whole lives in the ocean. This female turtle has come ashore only to lay her eggs.

Over on the rocks, I see a Sally Lightfoot crab. It is hard to make friends with them because whenever someone comes near, they hide in the cracks of the rocks.

Even though they are shy, these colorful crabs are fun to watch.

I love to look out at the huge ocean.
There are so many creatures in the water.
Stingrays, sharks, and squids all live right
in these waters.

I can see a sperm whale come up for air. Sperm whales can grow to be 60 feet (20 meters) long!

Closer to the shore, I can see some bottlenose dolphins. The dolphins don't mind the cold Galápagos waters because they have an extra layer of fat that helps to keep them warm. These fun friends communicate using whistles and clicks.

There is a blue-footed booby. It gets its silly name from the Spanish word *bobo*, which means "foolish." But these birds are serious hunters. They have excellent eyesight and breathe only through the corners of their mouths. These special qualities make diving for fish a lot easier.

This Galápagos frigate bird is resting with her chick before she goes out to find some food. They can fly farther out over the ocean than most other birds on the island.

When they catch a fish, they use their long hooked beaks. The males have beautiful red throat pouches that puff out like a bullfrog's when they want to show off.

Nearby, there is a large group of fur seals. They are much smaller than sea lions, and they are covered in a warm fur coat.

These furry friends have large families. They like to spend time together on the sand and rocks instead of swimming in the ocean.

A Galápagos finch is perched nearby. There are about 13 different types of finches in the Galápagos. While they all look similar, each type of finch has a different diet. They may look tiny, but these birds sure know how to survive!

This marine iguana is sunning on a rock.
These lizards like to go into the ocean,
where they find algae to eat. They can dive
and swim underwater for nearly 30 minutes
without taking a breath! Then they warm up
and dry off on the sun-soaked rocks.

From here, I see Galápagos penguins. They are the only type of penguins in the world that do not live in a cold climate.

It is hot on the Galápagos Islands, but the penguins love the cool ocean water.

Overhead, a waved albatross soars. She has just eaten a fish and is flying back to her nest on the lava rocks. She will probably warm her baby birds. I am headed over to the lava rocks, too. But she can fly much faster than I can walk.

On my way inland, I spot a Galápagos cormorant. While they have wings, these birds do not fly! Since there are no predators to hunt them, the birds do not need to fly in order to escape. The cormorants like to stay near the water and rarely travel inland.

Many animals make their homes on lava rocks near the Alcedo Volcano. There are a few families of waved albatrosses here. I also see a lava lizard.

Lava lizards like to soak up the heat from the warm rocks, but they can be found all over the island, not just on lava rocks. This lava lizard is warming up on a marine iguana's head!

I am getting hungry. On my way to find something to eat, I see a carpenter bee. This one is getting the nectar from a beautiful flower. Then she will fly back to her nest. Carpenter bees make their nests inside the wood of trees.

I have found something good to eat. There are lots of yummy plants on the Galápagos Islands. Tortoises love guavas, cacti, leaves, vines, and grass. Because there is so much water in these foods, we don't have to stop to drink very often. When I'm done with my meal, I will find more to eat. Tortoises like to eat up to 80 pounds (36 kilograms) a day.

It has been a long day. This sea lion is getting ready to sleep. I am tired as well.

We met so many cool Galápagos animals today. I will settle into a mud wallow to sleep. Good night!

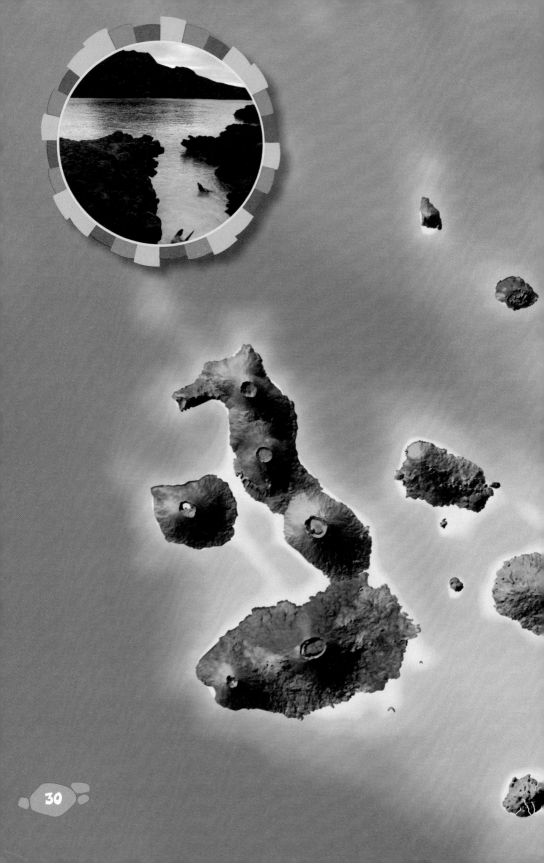

The Galápagos Islands are made up of 16 islands along the Equator. They are located nearly 600 miles (965 kilometers) from the nearest mainland of Ecuador in South America. Each island was created as the result of volcanic activity. Many of the volcanoes there are still active.

Glossary

Cold-blooded - An animal that is cold-blooded has an internal temperature that is changed by the temperature of its surroundings.

Climate - general long-term weather conditions of a specific area

Nectar - a sweet liquid found inside several flowers that some animals drink

Predators - animals that eat other animals

Wallow - a place where animals roll in the water or mud to cool themselves off